Draw and Color

Insects

Learn to draw and color 26 insects,
step by easy step, shape by simple shape!

Illustrated by Diana Fisher

Getting Started

When you **look** closely at the **drawings** in this book, you'll notice that they're made up of basic shapes, such as circles, triangles, and rectangles. To draw all your favorite creatures, just start with simple shapes as you see here. It's easy and fun!

Triangles can act as a base for a head.

Circles are a great way to start both spider heads and bodies.

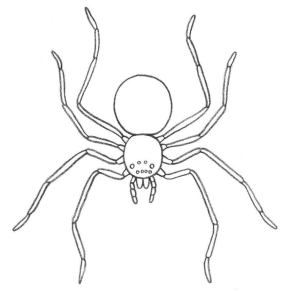

Ovals are perfect for insect heads and bodies— especially in profile.

Coloring Tips

There's more than one way to bring **creepy crawlies** to life on paper—you can use crayons, markers, or colored pencils. Be sure you have plenty of good "bug" colors—from black, brown, and green to bright red, blue, yellow, and orange!

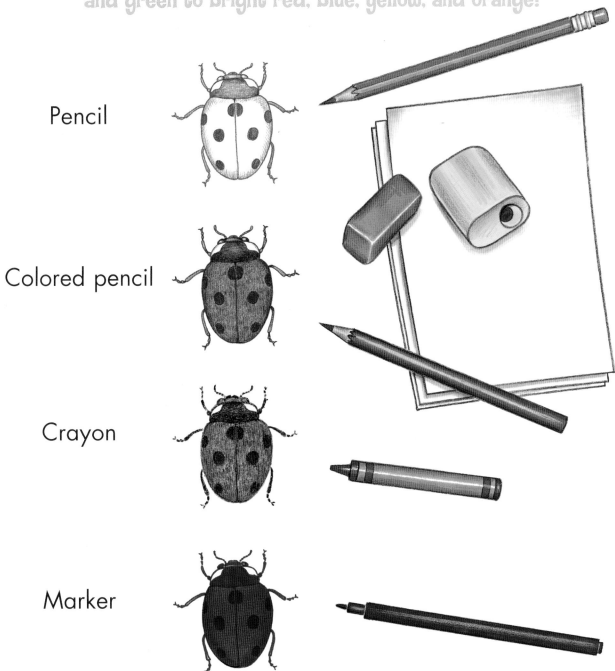

Pencil

Colored pencil

Crayon

Marker

Pill Millipede

Rolling up into a tight **ball** is what this bug does best! It hides its 15 pairs of legs and tucks in its head for protection.

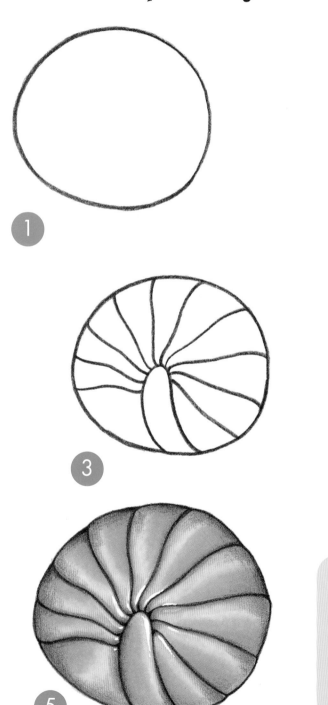

1

2

3

4

5

fun fact

Millipede means 1000 feet, but no millipede has more than 750 legs. Although large species of pill millipedes can grow to the size of a tennis ball, millipedes in this order have only 30 legs.

Walking Stick

This **slender** insect **disguises** itself among plants and trees. Brown coloring and a spiny, ridged body provide camouflage.

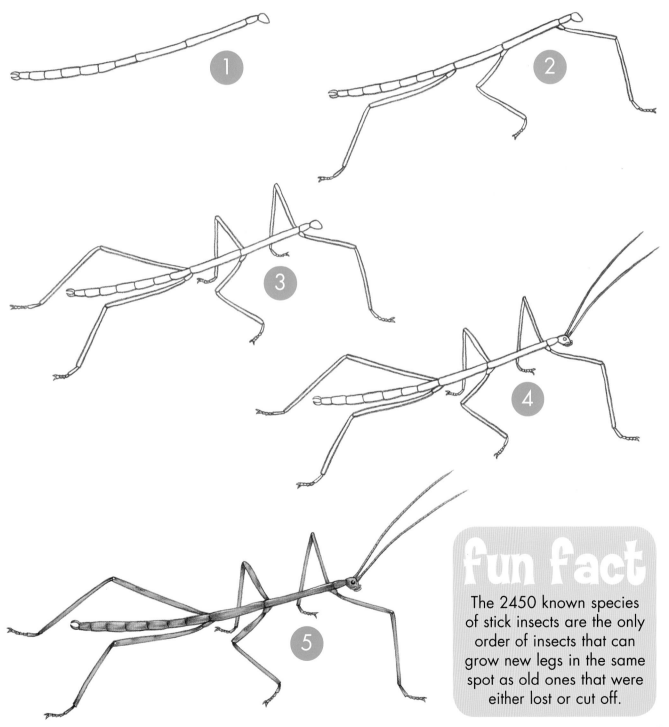

fun fact

The 2450 known species of stick insects are the only order of insects that can grow new legs in the same spot as old ones that were either lost or cut off.

Stink Bug

Bold colors warn would-be predators that this **shield** bug tastes foul—if the bug's signature smell doesn't scare them off first!

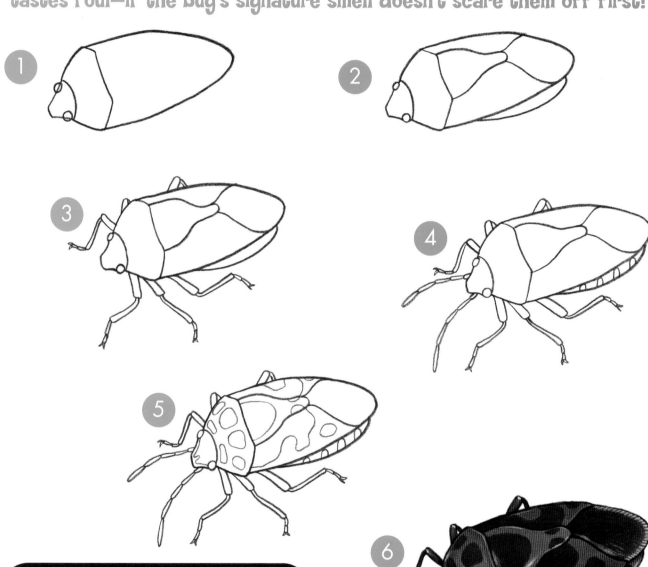

fun fact

Many bugs travel to warmer places in the winter because their bodies can't take the cold—but glycerol in the stink bug's bloodstream acts as an antifreeze, keeping its body from freezing in winter.

Treehopper

Also known as a **thorn** bug, the treehopper has a **unique** shape that provides a disguise and makes the bug difficult to eat!

Luna Moth

All "moon" moths possess large, **furry** bodies with **broad,** long-tailed wings. But only the male sports feathered antennae!

fun fact

This American saturnid moth species is named after the eyespots on its wings, which look like moons. It is alternately referred to as "luna," "lunar," and "moon" moth—all three names meaning exactly the same thing.

Spitting Spider

A **domed** body and symmetrical **spots** distinguish this arachnid—but its two large, spitting chelicerae are hard to ignore!

1

2

3

4

5

6

fun fact

This spider doesn't spin webs. Instead it spits a sticky, gluelike substance, moving its two projecting chelicerae back and forth to stop its prey in its tracks!

Broad-Winged Damselfly

Features like its **round** eyes and **slender** body are dragonfly-like, but the damsel's folded wing pairs are all its own!

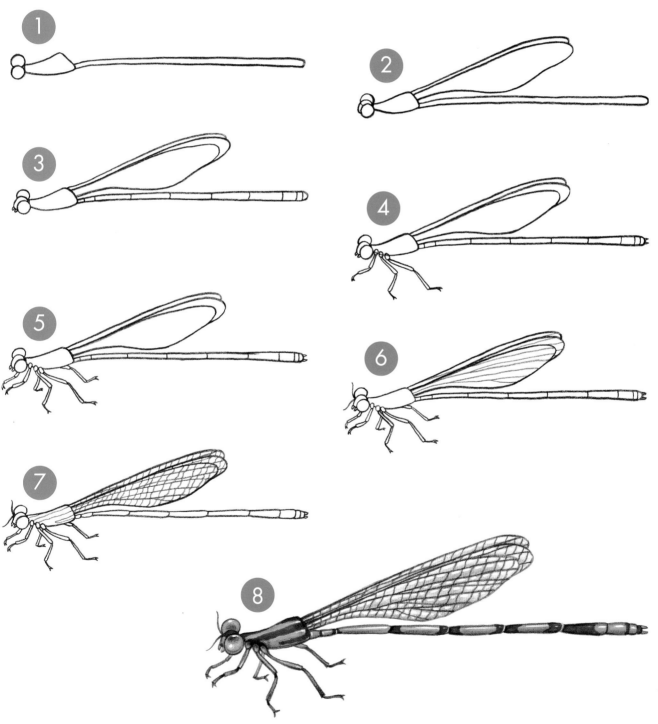

Chactid Scorpion

Pinching **claws** and a **stinging** tail separate this arachnid from its spider cousins, despite its pedipalps and eight legs.

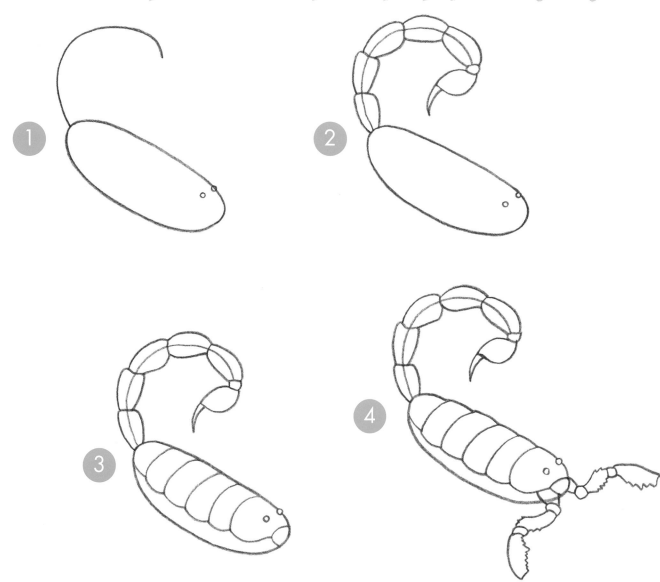

fun fact Scorpions are famous for venomous stings—but out of 1400 species of scorpions, only about two dozen are truly dangerous to humans. The chactidae family have a beelike sting, harmless unless an allergic reaction occurs.

Fire Ant

The fire ant's **bumpy** tapered "**waist**" connects its upper body—or thorax—to its abdomen, where its stinger is located.

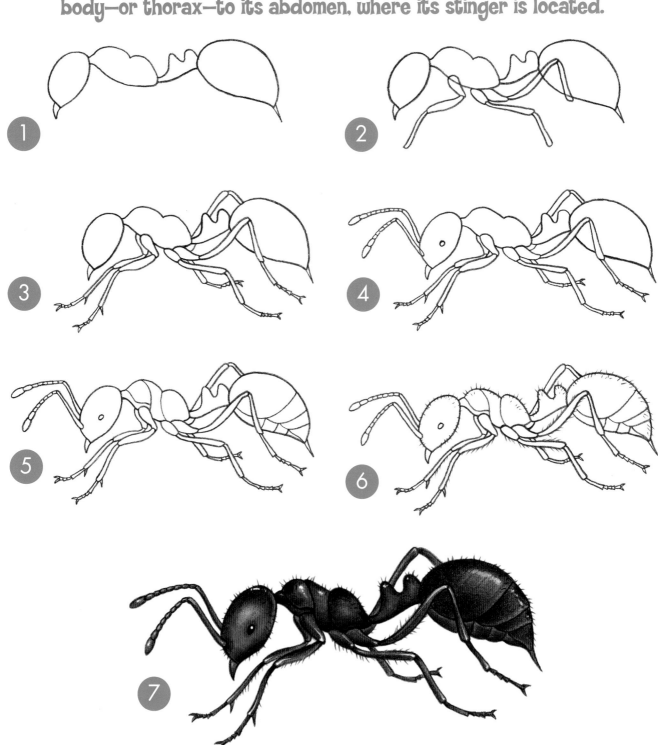

Higher Termite

The **pale** snouted harvester termite has a **dark,** round head with a long, nozzlelike end. The worker has antennae but no eyes!

Scutigerid Centipede

This predator has **large, compound** eyes and poison claws. It's born with 14 legs and gains a new pair after each molt.

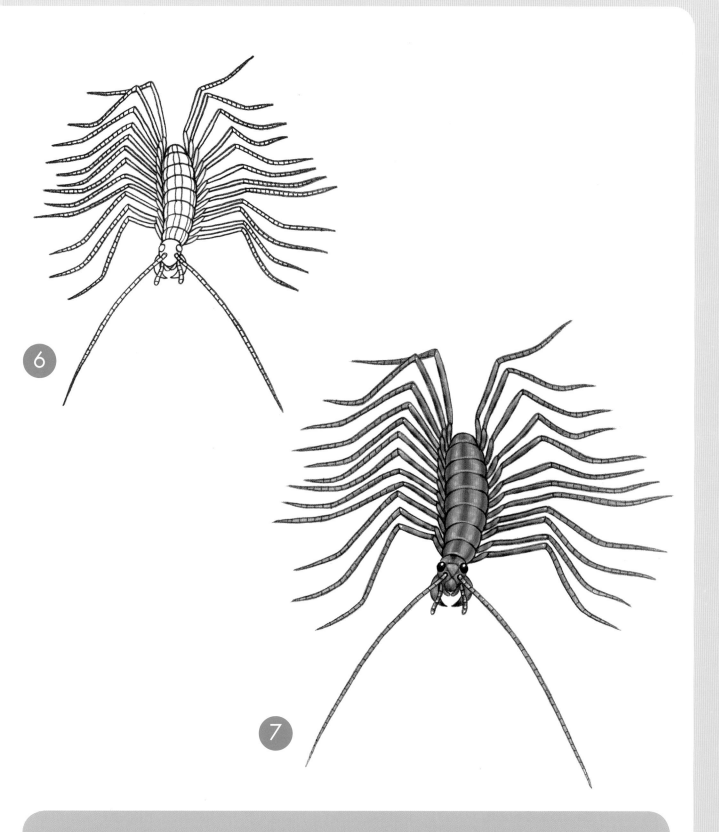

6

7

Life Stages

All animals **change** as they **grow.** But some insects experience major changes in appearance as they develop over time!

The honeybee starts out as an egg, laid by the queen. Once hatched, the egg becomes a pale, grublike larva. In the final larval stage, the bee is still pale, but closer to its final shape, which it reaches after 21 days.

The lightning bug, or firefly, develops from an egg into a wingless larva called a "glow worm." After eating for about three months, the larva digs a tunnel. Later it emerges from the ground as a fully developed beetle.

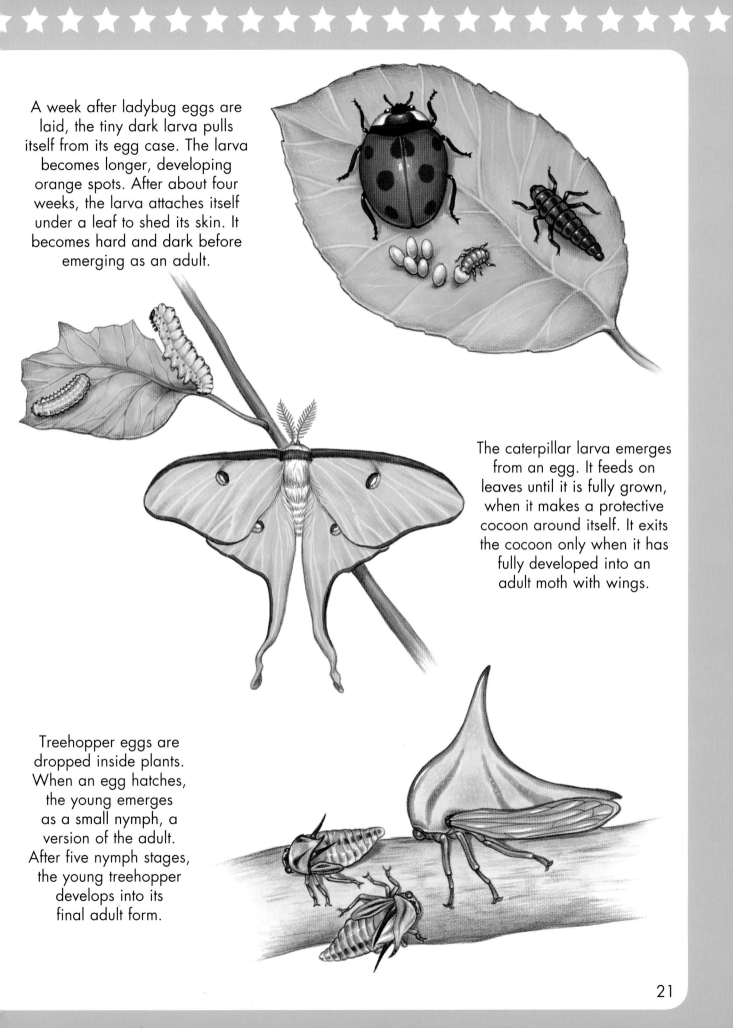

A week after ladybug eggs are laid, the tiny dark larva pulls itself from its egg case. The larva becomes longer, developing orange spots. After about four weeks, the larva attaches itself under a leaf to shed its skin. It becomes hard and dark before emerging as an adult.

The caterpillar larva emerges from an egg. It feeds on leaves until it is fully grown, when it makes a protective cocoon around itself. It exits the cocoon only when it has fully developed into an adult moth with wings.

Treehopper eggs are dropped inside plants. When an egg hatches, the young emerges as a small nymph, a version of the adult. After five nymph stages, the young treehopper develops into its final adult form.

21

Jewel Wasp

Known for its dimpled, **hard** body with **metallic** coloring, this bright jewel of the bug world is also known as a "ruby-tailed wasp."

Fulgorid Bug

For a master of **camouflage**, this **odd** bug with a unique head shape sure stands out! It startles predators with its bright wings.

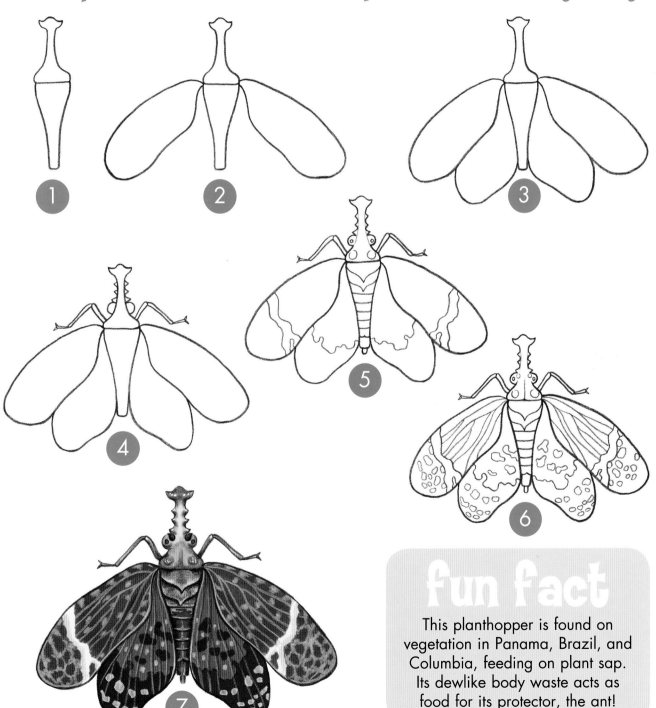

23

Leaf Beetle

A **shiny** shell and **flexible** black legs make the sagra species look almost robotic! Its nickname is the jeweled frog beetle.

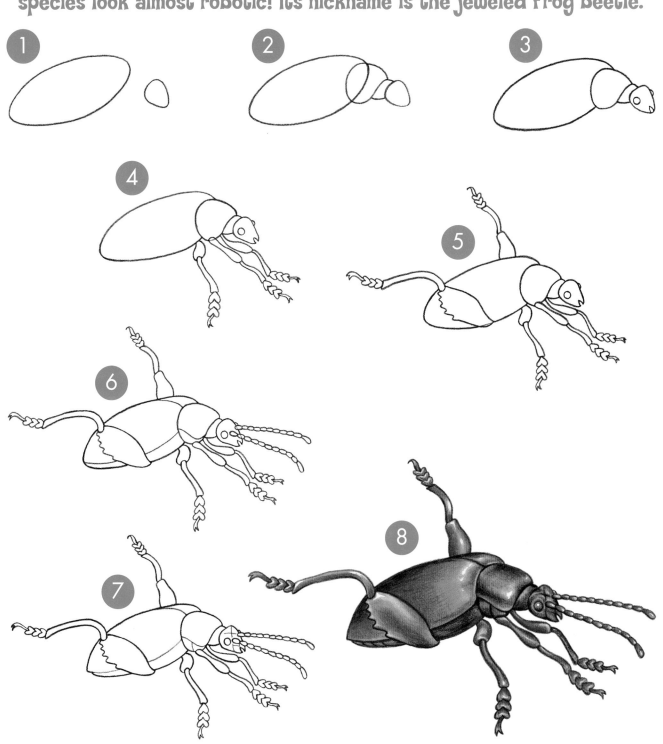

Acanthosomatid Bug

A **Y-shaped** mark on its thorax **distinguishes** this bug from other species with small heads and shield shapes!

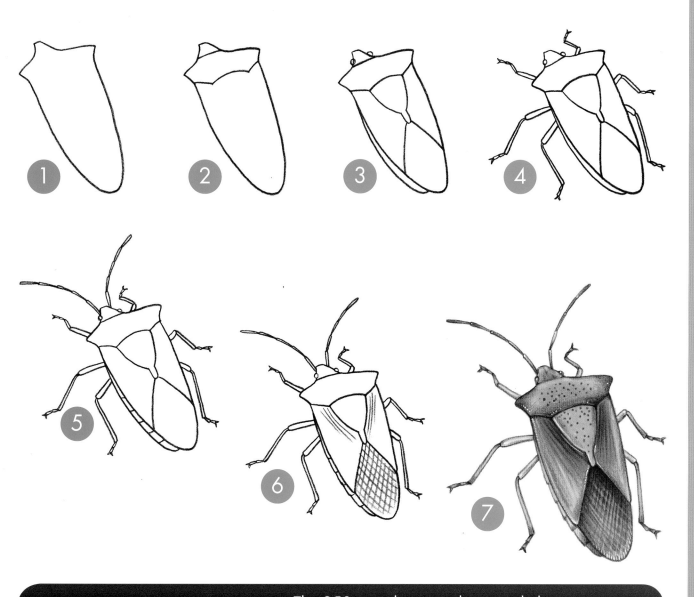

fun fact

The 250 acanthosomatid species belong to an order of 82,000 species. Only these animals are considered true *bugs*. The other 1,055,00 species of *arthropods* includes other types of insects, spiders, moths, and all the rest of what we commonly call "bugs."

Praying Mantis

Natural coloring and **leafy** wings camouflage the mantis, while large eyes, sharp leg spines, and powerful jaws capture its prey.

1

2

3

4

5

6

7

fun fact

Legend has it that the female praying mantis always eats the male mantis after mating. It's true that females will sometimes eat mates—especially if in captivity—but most males are *not* eaten by their partners.

Common Scorpionfly

Narrow, banded wings, a **beaked** head, and a slender body distinguish this bug. The male's abdomen has a scorpionlike tip.

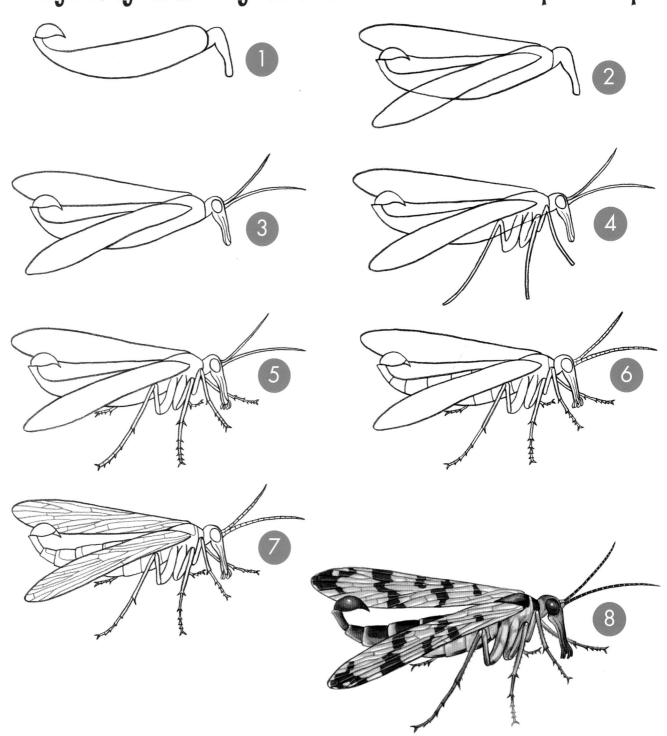

Katydid

With **short** wings, long legs, and **bright** green coloring, this bush cricket bears a strong resemblance to a grasshopper!

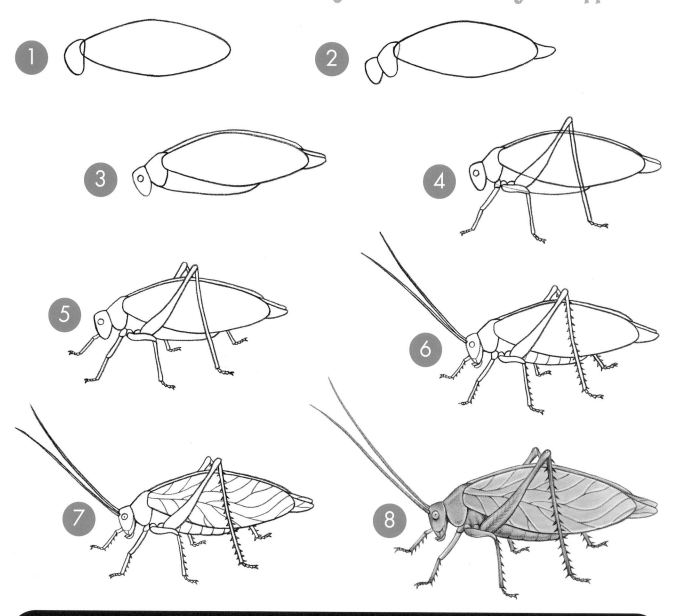

1
2
3
4
5
6
7
8

fun fact

The katydid is named for the sound it makes, a call that sounds like "katy did." Male katydids "sing" with the base of their front wings to attract mates, and females respond with a soft song of their own. These songs are heard through "eardrums" located in the katydid's front legs!

Violin Beetle

Long and **flat**, this member of the **ground** beetle set gets its common name from its head and body outline.

1

2

3

4

5

6

7

8

Cicada

The magicicada species features **red** eyes and **orange** wing veins. Its tapered abdomen shape amplifies its music!

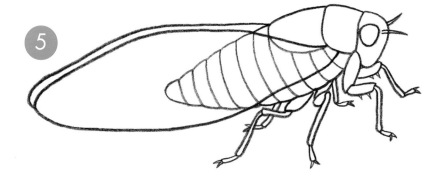

fun fact

Groups of magicicada adults emerge in the United States at 13- and 17-year intervals, depending on the brood. After hatching, the young cicadas drop from the trees and crawl underground, where they spend years developing!

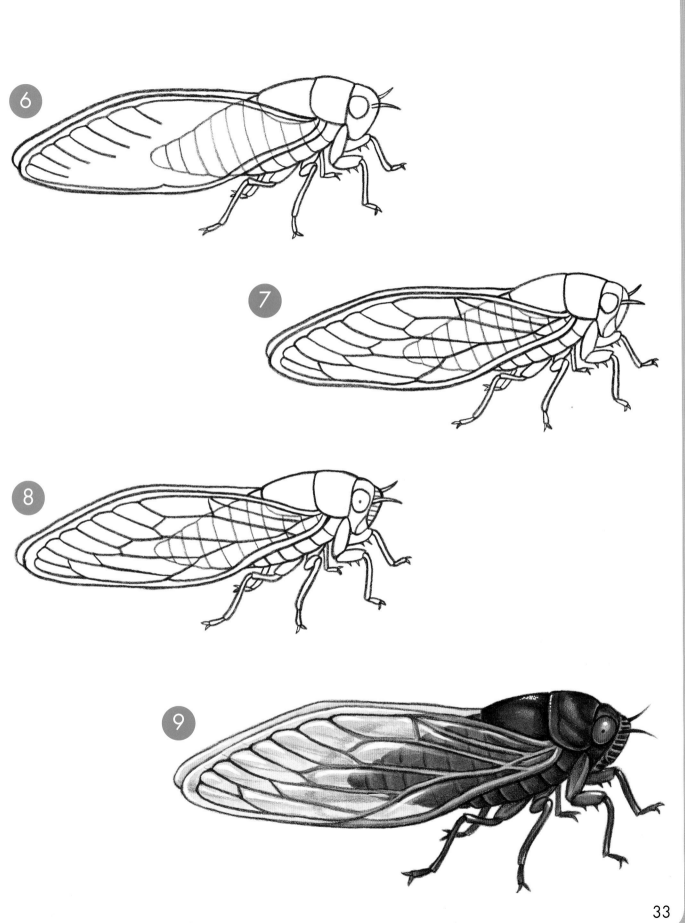

6

7

8

9

33

Yellow Jacket Wasp

All social wasps have **tiny** waists and **warning** coloration, such as the bright yellow patches that cover this species' black body.

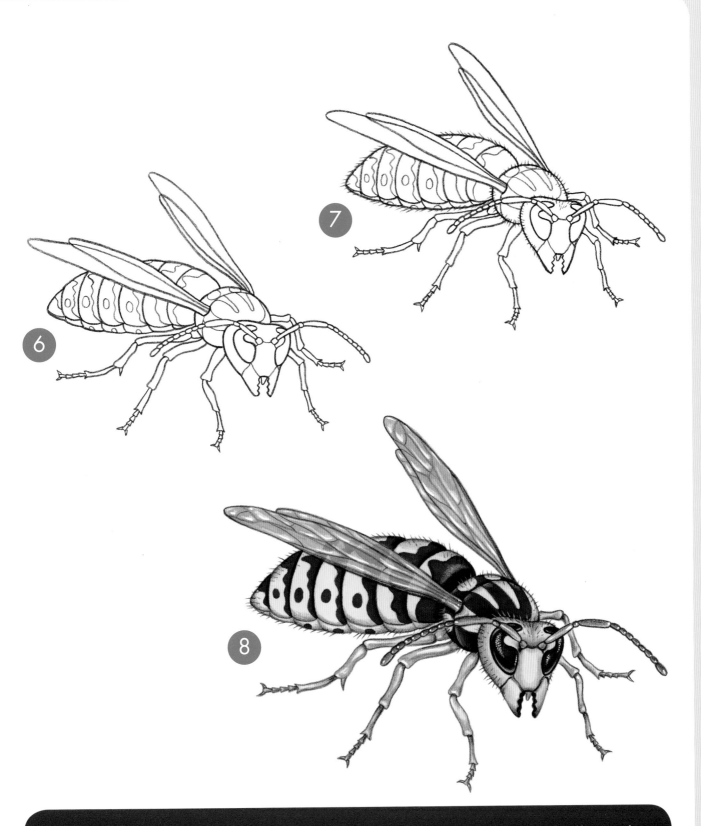

fun fact

The comblike cells of a wasp nest are used to house the wasp eggs and larvae. But because the cells face down and open at the bottom, the queen must glue her eggs inside the cells to keep them from falling out!

Solpugid

A type of **sun spider,** this desert-dweller has a hairy body, big chelicerae that act as pincers, and pedipalps with suction pads!

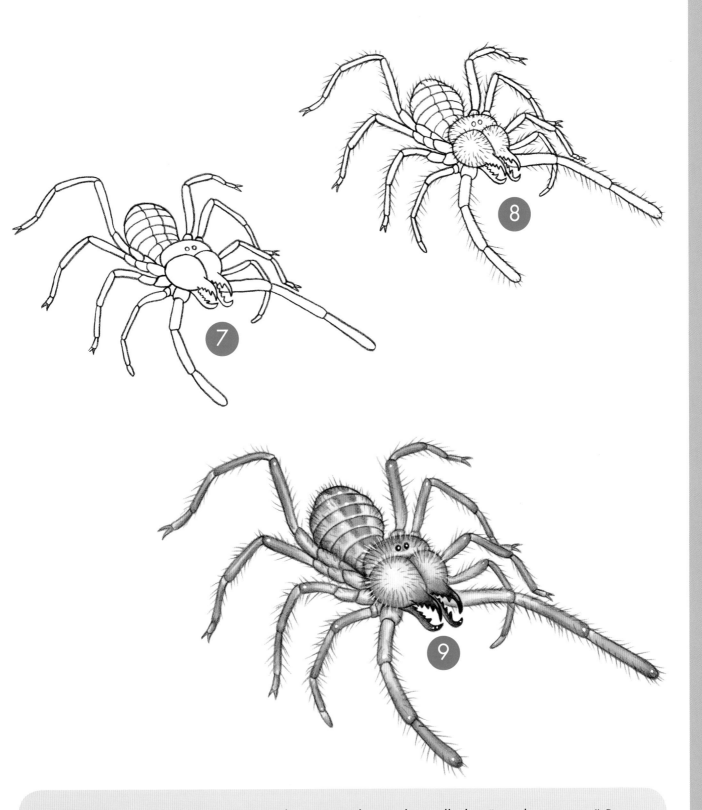

fun fact

The sun spider is also called a "wind scorpion." But despite its names and resemblances, this animal is not related to spiders, scorpions, or other arachnids. It's part of its own order, solifugae, which includes 1000 species.

Lace Bug

A distinct, lacy **wing** pattern gives this small **gray** bug its name. A lacelike plate even extends to hood its head!

8

9

10

11

12

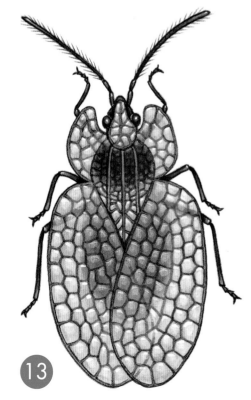

13

Western Honey Bee

One of the **smaller** bees, this slender, slightly **hairy** insect is the best known of the honey bees—and it is now found worldwide.

fun fact

The honeybee is the most domesticated insect because of its ability to make—what else?—honey. To make one jar of honey, worker bees make millions of trips between flowers—where they collect nectar—and the hive, where they store their food.